CHURCH BOARD

TIPS AND RESOURCES TO BUILD A STRONG
BIBLICAL CHURCH BOARD

Bryan Walker, PhD

TABLE OF CONTENTS

Chapter 1: (Re)Building the Foundation 8
TIP # 1 8
The Church 10
The Board 15
Deacons and Elders 19
Resources for You 24

Chapter 2: How Does Your Church Board Function? 25
TIP # 2 25
3 Typical Board Designs 26
Barriers that Church Boards Face 28
The Decision-Making Process.. 30
How does your church leadership make decisions? 32
What decision-making types help create healthy church leadership teams? 36
Resources for You 37

Chapter 3: Church Boards: They Need to Be Better! (Part 1) .. 38
TIP #3 38
The Tension of Organizational Structure......................... 39
Something Better... 42
Healthy Tension.. 47
Resources for You 49

Chapter 4: Church Boards – They Need to be Better! (Part 2) 52
TIP #4 52
Unfortunate Attitudes 52
We GET to do this!.. 56
Your Board and Your Congregation 58
Creating a Purpose Statement for Your Board................. 61
Resources for You 65

Chapter 5: Spiritual Maturity and Church Leadership 66

TIP #5 .... *66*
The Doctrine of Sanctification 67
The Doctrine of Spiritual Maturity 68
Spiritual Fruit 69
Resources for You... 72

Chapter 6: The Ideal Relationship: "A More Perfect Union" .. 74

TIP #6 .... *74*
RISE UP – and Pray Like King David! 75
Resources for you. 78

References 80

ABOUT THE AUTHOR

Bryan Walker has served in leadership in a Fortune 500 company, as well as business leadership in restaurant franchising. Outside of the for-profit business world, Bryan has served in top leadership in a healthcare organization, a Christian school, and a Christian university. Currently, he is the president of a national network of churches.

Bryan holds a bachelor's degree in business from Grand Valley State University, a master's degree in Nonprofit Organizational Management from Western Michigan University, and a Ph.D. in Nonprofit Organizational Management and Ministry Leadership from Liberty University.

In addition to the academic and vocational journeys he has taken to sharpen his understanding of nonprofit leadership, Bryan has also had the privilege to serve on church boards and nonprofit boards for over twenty-five years in capacities within the committees of treasury, funding and development, operations, executive, and board excellence.

Throughout his faith journey and spiritual growth, Bryan developed a passion for serving the church. Meeting during their years of high school, Bryan and his wife, Ami, were married 1990 and have three adult daughters, three sons-in-law, and (at the writing of this book) five amazing grandchildren.

INTRODUCTION

I'm a church board nerd! I am fascinated by church boards, having spent much of my adult life serving on, studying, and supporting church boards. I am passionate about helping board members become the very best they can be in their role. I sincerely believe the church board is the first line of defense against Satan's attacks against churches, and that a strong, healthy, biblical church board—full of spiritually healthy church board members—can repel those attacks.

Being a "church board member" is significantly different than any other role on a non-profit or for-profit board that you might serve. Yes, there are some similar skills that carry over from those other non-church boards into the church board room, but it is safe to say to you that being a church board member is like nothing else you'll ever do. I applaud you for answering God's call to serve as a board member in your church. In addition to your ministry on the board, you likely volunteer in other areas at your church while also working 40+ hours each week, helping raise your family, and being involved in your community. Your willingness to answer the high call of a church board member deserves special reverence and recognition.

You're highly motivated, but likely untrained. Most church board members that I've met across the country (including me at one point) often don't truly understand the role, but they strongly desire to do their very best.

The issue is not motivation. The issue is typically unawareness.

You've heard that you can bring a horse to water, but you can't make it drink. But this old adage isn't finished. There's one more sentence that goes along with it: While you can't make it drink, you can make it thirsty. When someone understands that what you're trying to do is help them, they might just lean into what you offer and invest themselves into it. I've found two questions which help people see their need to make an investment:

- **WHAT is the biblical role of a church board member and how it is an essential part of their church?** Knowing that God has designed and defined the role of a church board member—and that it isn't just a casual task asked of the naturally gifted leaders in a church—inspires many to focus on their own growth and development.
- **WHY be a better church board member?** When you can see the potential impact you could make on the pastor, church, and its mission as an excellent board member, your motivation to learn and grow becomes essential. It's no different than church musicians who practices, sometimes daily, to hone their skills. Church board members must remain committed to growing their gifts to serve in their ministry role.

As you accept the high call to serve on your church board, I invite you to invest important time and energy into the short, easy-to-read, chapters of this book. It will be a good investment for you, your pastor, your fellow board members, and the congregation of your church.

God's blessings on you in your faithful service to Him as a member on your church board!

Dr. Bryan J. Walker

1

(RE)BUILDING THE FOUNDATION

TIP # 1

UNDERSTAND AND EMBRACE THE BIBLICAL ROLE OF LEADERSHIP IN YOUR CHURCH

Untrained or *under-trained*? *"The board member is the least trained volunteer in the church,"* a good friend once told me. Ugh. It was convicting to hear, but the more that I work with churches across the country, the more I believe that he was right. While church board members may have leadership competencies, that doesn't necessarily mean they are more equipped to serve on a church board than, say, a person who likes to eat delicious food would be considered a chef. Well experienced leaders are not necessarily ready (or even qualified) to serve on a church board.

The board member is the least trained volunteer in the church.

Hear me out. While experience and education may get us some positions right away, other positions require training. A person who flies frequently for work becomes comfortable with planes and air travel, but unless they've been to flight school—and passed—they're wholly unprepared to actually fly a plane. It takes specific training, regardless of the degree of comfort or confidence.

It's the same with church boards. We might have leadership competency, but it might not directly apply to what we will be called to do for our churches. In fact, it's entirely possible that some high-capacity, well-experienced leaders are not at all equipped for serving on a church board. Churches should intentionally seek people who are not necessarily leaders.

We NEED to know. The incredible privilege of serving on a board of a church requires us to fully understand what it means to be a church board member. We are blessed to have God's specific instructions already written for us in Scripture. This task is so essentially important to the church that God Himself defined it. Of the many things we can do with our life both vocationally and in our volunteering, serving on a church board is one of the most clearly defined by God.

Spiritual maturity. Of the expectations and character qualities of deacons and elders, the most essential is that the person must have outstanding spiritual maturity. A problem is that to many, spiritual maturity is personal and private ("Who are you to ask?"). Or it's difficult to understand and describe ("I'm not entirely sure how to describe it..."). These problems are especially true in the church board room. Church board members are often long-term friends and acquaintances, and our willingness to 'dig in' and ask important questions about our co-leaders can be easily overlooked. Additionally, because of those long-time relationships, we might be inclined to avoid confronting behaviors or attitudes that reveal spiritual concerns.

To learn more about the importance and definition of spiritual maturity, take a look at Chapter 5, titled "*Spiritual Maturity and Church Leadership*" in this book.

But first, let's take a quick look at the basics.

The Church

Okay, first: I'm not attempting to define "The Church" or The Body of Christ or what it should be. That work is done in detail in many great books. My goal is simply to present a basic and simple foundation of what you and I call "our church."

An Organism or Organization? I've heard it said that "A church is an *organism*, not an *organization*." In my experience, this argument happens when someone rejects a church's organizational structure.

So, what's the answer—organism or organization? The seemingly impossible answer is YES to both if it's done in a healthy way. Or NO to both if it's unhealthy. Here is a basic definition of each.

- **An Organism.** This word is used to say the church is meant to be organic—something that looks and feels like it's easily-adaptable. It grows (or shrinks) based on the needs of the people. Unstructured to the eye, a church that is a healthy organism functions with order and peace, similar to a healthy pond in your backyard. It features friendly and well-respected relationships. Any hierarchy or rulebook, like the constitution or bylaws, is subtle and functions silently in the background.

- **An Organization.** When this word is used to describe a church, it's often done with negativity—a critique rather than a compliment. Specifically, it describes a formally-structured church, designed with a constitution and bylaws. It can feel a bit rigid and inflexible, following rules and with a clear leadership structure.

	What it looks like in a **Healthy** Church	What it looks like in an **Unhealthy** Church
An **Organism**	*The church:* - Has a clear mission and purpose and pursues them both fully and joyfully. - Is ready and able to accommodate visitors. - Is easily adaptable to the needs of the congregation. - Has ministries that are relevant and functional. - Serves its congregation fully. - Seeks ways to serve the community. - With church discipline – it follows the biblical model.	*The church:* - Has an unclear understanding of its mission and purpose. It is more like a social club or small group. - Seems to miss opportunities to fully serve its people. - Is unable to connect with or host visitors. - Has one or two ministries but does not adapt to the needs of its congregation. - With church discipline – it follows a model that feels popular or most-desired.

An **Organization**	*The church:* <ul><li>Can function comfortably within its defined mission and purpose.</li><li>Uses its official documents to help support the ministry.</li><li>Feels warm and welcoming to visitors.</li><li>Is transparent and appropriate in decision-making.</li><li>Has a clear leadership structure that follows the biblical design of church leadership.</li><li>With church discipline – it follows the biblical model as defined in its bylaws with grace and love.</li></ul>	*The church:* <ul><li>Functions with rigidity and coldness as it follows its official documents.</li><li>Feels cold or unwelcoming to visitors.</li><li>The leadership makes decisions in private and does not offer transparency or congregational involvement.</li><li>Does not show biblical love and/or grace.</li><li>With church discipline – it follows the model as defined in its bylaws, but with a clear lack of grace and love.</li></ul>

Practically speaking, a church will move through seasons with varying degrees of tension or imbalance. Sometimes it's more of an organism, and at other times, more of an organization.

For example, when a new church is just starting and people are still trying to figure things out, the church might feel much more like an organism. Without much structure or design, a healthy new church will feature people working together.

Conversely, a more mature church that has been in ministry for many years and is healthy might tend to carry more attributes of an organization. It may use its formal structure to build creativity and strength throughout its established ministries and outreach.

The health and feel – or internal culture – of a church is a direct reflection of its leadership.

Church leadership (the pastor and board) is significantly responsible for how the church wrestles with its structure, defining how it functions and serves its congregation—as an organization or organism. Leadership also determines if the church functions in a healthy or unhealthy way. In the many churches that I have served and researched, <u>the health and feel -or internal culture- of a church is a direct reflection of its leadership.</u> That inspires me to learn more about church leadership and to prayerfully and actively pursue growing in it.

I believe it can inspire you as well.
Let's dive a bit deeper together.

The Board

When we use the word *"board"* in church leadership, it's typically for two basic and commonly understood reasons:

1) It's the word the Christian church has primarily used for the team who serve and lead the church along with the pastor.

2) It's also the word that most nonprofit organizations and non-government organizations (NGOs) use for the team who serve and lead the organization along with the CEO.

We use the word *board* because we're familiar with it. But being familiar with the word and understanding its role in the church are two very different things.

Calling the group of leaders in the church a board is not a problem, per se. The word itself is not un-biblical. But it can create confusion. We're used to it, and it's common in the marketplace. But in our churches, there should be a clear difference between a church board and a nonprofit board. Because a church board is not a nonprofit board.

Here's where the tension exists. Churches take on the appearance and attributes of a nonprofit or for-profit organization. We typically do what we do because we know what we know. In other words, we tend to duplicate what we do in the marketplace's boardroom to what we do in our church's boardroom. Then in turn, our churches begin to operate like a marketplace organization. And for many, if not most churches, that's a significant problem.

It MUST be different. Our church boards need to be different than that of a nonprofit organization's board, or any other type of leadership. **If your church board looks, feels, functions, is structured like, uses similar terminology as any type of leadership or board that you're familiar with outside of the Bible's specific design, drop it and start over. Build something new.**

"Bryan, are you saying that nothing good can come from taking leadership design or principles from the marketplace?"

Definitely not! I have invested deeply in learning about and following best practices in organizational leadership. But with our inclination to do what we do because we know what we know, we will always gravitate toward what we're most comfortable with. We won't (and probably shouldn't) truly remove all elements of our non-church leadership experience from the church boardroom. But finding proper balance, we must press harder into imitating the Bible's defined process of church leadership by shedding our inclinations to use organizational leadership practices.

This chart gives a quick look at the basic differences between a church board and a nonprofit board.

	Church Board	**Nonprofit Board**
What drives the organization	Following the biblical design of the Church	Mission and goal accomplishment
Organizational structure	Collaborative, following the spiritual leadership of the elders and pastor	Hierarchical (Board, CEO, Exec. Team, etc.)
Decision-making process	Led by the pastor, elders and deacons, collaborative with congregation	Follows the process described in the bylaws
Board members	Equal and collaborative with the pastor, spiritual leaders of the church, spiritually mature who meet the biblical qualifications	Individuals who possess gifts or resources that have positive impact on the mission of the organization

To make this even more simple, I suggest using this simple Question & Answer Test with your church board:

If your church board does this…	*Then do this…*
Spends significant time in your board meetings on decisions like paint colors, contractor budgets, finance concerns, etc. **instead of** shepherding your congregation…	**Invert it.** Shepherd first—and maybe *only,* especially if you don't have time for other tasks. Work on stewarding assets second. Let the lawn grow and the paint fade —just don't sacrifice the shepherding of your congregation.
Spends significant time in your board meetings on project management issues **instead of** praying over your pastor and finding ways to support him…	**Invert it.** Pray over and care for your pastor first; work on caring for your properties and grounds second. Satan viciously hates your pastor and continuously attacks him on every front of his life. Your pastor needs your prayer-filled support and protection.
Spends significant time on managing your church's budget, investment account, or checkbook **instead of** learning about and protecting your church's doctrine…	**Invert it.** Work together to become scholars of Scripture and your church's doctrinal statement. Prayerfully seek ways to communicate it and to protect it.

Spends significant time on your pastoral search process or dreaming of a larger congregation **instead of** embracing your current situation…	**Invert it.** Encourage each other and your congregation that God loves your church and His timing and plan for your church is already defined—glorifying Him—and learn how to embrace your church's current situation.

While I don't advocate to remove all elements of a nonprofit or for-profit board from the church board process, I do recommend that you follow the Scripture's design for your church board, not the marketplace design. That might simply start by dropping the name Board and calling it something different, like Council or Leadership Team. Just to help break the mold and to start new.

Before we go much further, it's essential to understand the two basic positions Scripture defines for church leadership: deacons and elders. Many of us still use these titles and they're basically the same titles the New Testament Christians used as described in the Apostle Paul's letters.

Deacons and Elders

DEACONS – while views differ between churches and regions, we can largely agree on some basics. Deacons are:

- **The stewards _of_ the church.** This includes having oversight of the finances (fiduciary), campus and facilities.
- **The relationship-builders _within_ the church.** This includes inviting and greeting visitors, caring for staff and volunteers, and strengthening relationships within the congregation.

ELDERS – this role is considered to run parallel to the pastor, commonly referred to as the plurality of ministry. Elders:

- *Co-Shepherd _with_ the Pastor.* This includes caring for the spiritual needs of the members of the congregation and helping to advance the Gospel and the church's mission.
- *Caregiver of the Pastor.* This includes tending to the spiritual, physical, relational, and vocational needs of the pastor.
- *One of the key differences* – and maybe the *only* difference – between the role of a deacon and that of an elder, as described in 1 Timothy 3:2 and 1 Peter 5:2, is that the elder needs to be able and well-prepared to teach authoritatively on biblical truth and to provide biblical oversight of the teaching within the church.

It's important to note the biblical differences in these roles. As noted in Strauch's *Biblical Eldership* (2003), the author highlights Neil Summerton, from his book, *A Noble Task: Eldership and Ministry in the Local Church* (1987). He states:

"...to both Timothy and Titus, Paul is crystal clear that the indispensable quality, which incidentally distinguishes the elder from the deacon, is the ability to master Christian doctrine, to evaluate it in others, to teach it, and to debate it with those who teach falsehood (1 Timothy 3:2; Titus 1:9-16)."

Deacon and elder roles are meant to complement and support each other with their own assigned and defined tasks. Neither better nor more influential than the other. The biblical qualifications for these roles are clear and similar (see 1 & 2 Timothy and Titus), and outstanding books have been written on this topic, listed in the resources for this chapter.

The danger of not knowing: Wolves in the Pen. The Apostle Paul stated: "I know that after my departure fierce wolves will come in among you, not sparing the flock" (Acts 20:29). His warning is clear: Be careful of who you trust with the biblical leadership in your church! In fact, here is the full warning that Paul spoke to the elders of the church in Ephesus:

"Pay careful attention to yourselves and to all the flock, in which the Holy Spirit has made you overseers, to care for the church of God, which he obtained with his own blood. I know that after my departure fierce wolves will come in among you, not sparing the flock; and from among your own selves will arise men speaking twisted things, to draw away the disciples after them." (Acts 20:28-29)

Thinking practically about this sheep and wolf metaphor—it means that church leaders need to be extra cautious as they serve and lead their church. People will come to divide and fight with selfish and ungodly intentions. But there's a more subtle warning:

- *A natural predator.* A wolf doesn't know it's a wolf; it just knows it's hungry, and sheep are easy prey. Wolves don't choose to be predators. It's what they are. I met a man who domesticates purebred wolves. His gentle dogs were enormous predators, but gentle as a golden retriever. All this to say, a wolf can be trained to be something different than its nature.
- *<u>We</u> are the wolves!* We don't choose to be sinners, it's what we are. Yes, when we accept Christ as our Savior, we are made new and are no longer enslaved to our old selves. But our sinful nature can still drive us to be destructive even when we don't intend to be. It requires us to be intentional and prayerful to *not* follow our sinful nature. Even the Apostle Paul struggled with this very thing when he said "but I am of the flesh, sold under sin. For I do not understand my own actions. For I do not do what I want, but I do the very thing I hate" (Romans 7:14-15).
- *Praise God!* Scripture shows us, in Romans 6, that we have victory over sin through the death, burial, and resurrection of Jesus Christ. But Paul's warning shows us we must be always diligent in the fight against sin.

Without that faithful fight, we can become a wolf in the pen. Don't underestimate the damage you can cause as a church board member.

Our sinful nature is extremely creative, and the evil destruction and hate that we can bring is extraordinary—especially within the church. Just like the Apostle Paul, we must fight against that sinful tendency. One of the more subtle weapons the enemy deploys is ignorance. The Oxford Dictionary defines ignorance as "the lack of knowledge or information." Even with the greatest of intentions, our ignorance can be destructive—especially for leaders who have influence and authority. The greatest defense we have against ignorance is the humble dedication to learning.

A warning for all church board members. My friends, I cannot stress it enough. It is essential that we understand the biblical roles we carry as we serve in church board leadership. Study. Pray. Hold each other accountable. Dedicate yourself to learning what your role means from a biblical perspective. Never stop seeking ways to improve and grow. Your hard work as you focus on this role will not be in vain.

Resources for You

<u>Helpful books to read:</u>

If you desire to dive deeply into the Biblical definitions and descriptions of these roles, I suggest reading these excellent books on church boards:

- *"Elders in the Life of the Church"* (Newton, Schmucker)
- *"High Impact Church Boards"* (Addington)
- *"Biblical Eldership"* (Strauch)

<u>Your notes:</u>

2

HOW DOES YOUR CHURCH BOARD FUNCTION?

TIP # 2

UNDERSTAND HOW YOUR CHURCH LEADERSHIP
PROCESS FUNCTIONS.

I've met with many church boards, and I am continually humbled by the servant-hearted people who faithfully lead and give of their valuable time to meet, plan, and work alongside their pastor in their church. I have yet to encounter a church board member who serves with an angry heart, but I've met many who simply are uninformed about how to serve as an elder or deacon in a biblical way.

I have yet to encounter a church board member who serves with an angry heart, but I've met many who simply are uninformed.

On the contrary, I have met several hundred board members who love Jesus and serve Him selflessly. The following observations are an accumulation of the basic board styles, and I describe them with the highest respect and admiration for the many board members who serve on them.

That said, I've found that church boards tend to be one of the following:

3 Typical Board Designs

(1) ***Combined.*** The board combines the roles of the deacons and elders into a single board. The church's constitution or bylaws might require a certain minimum number of elders and deacons, but rather than keeping the groups separate, they simply combine everyone into one group. These boards function more like a single deacon/elder board.

> *What does this type of board look like?* When you step into their board meetings, it's difficult to see the difference in roles between the board members ("Is he a deacon or elder?"). Or, there is no difference in their roles because they all do the same thing and its members might actually state it: "We all serve in the same role." They meet as a single group versus having separate meetings for the deacons and elders.

(2) ***Confused.*** The board is not fully certain about the differences between the elders and deacons, so this type of board will often function in a way that meets the efforts of its members. Similar to the Combined board, these boards meet in a single

group and the board members don't have different roles. The defining element of these boards is their board members don't understand their roles, so there is confusion and frustration among its members.

> *What does this type of board look like?* When you step into their board meetings, either there is a general discouragement among its members because of the confusion of its purpose, or its members can't see the board's inability to function properly. Board members often say things like "I think we're pretty healthy as a board because we get things done, we never argue, and we love our pastor and church."

(3) ***Compact.*** Because the church congregation is limited in size, the board is also small (3-5 members) and the group combines simply because of its size. While these boards are often both combined and confused, they also deal with the issue of not having enough members.

> *What does this type of board look like?* When you step into their board meetings, these members are the faithful few who have served diligently—often for decades—and attempt to balance the many needs of their church. There is no separation of roles because there are only a few of them. These board members often say things like "If we separate, there will only be a few elders and a few deacons; we can get more done by staying together."

This Tip focuses on the need to keep the roles of elder and deacon distinct and different as much as possible. A lack of clarity creates the tendency for these roles to be combined, confused, and compact. This is not an indictment of recklessness, but a call to awareness.

Barriers that Church Boards Face

In addition to the three different types of boards, I've also found a few key barriers which boards face as they go about making improvements. Here are two that are most common:

BARRIER 1: Adjusting and improving a church board is complicated. Church board members conclude their church is operating the best it can given the current circumstances. Sometimes churches experience a major crisis (like the unexpected departure of the pastor, an ethical failure by a person in the church, a facility problem, or a major financial concern, etc.), and the church board is barely hanging on. Yet those faithful board members somehow stay and work together. Asking anything more from them would simply be too much. Unfortunately, small churches face this reality too often. I thank God for board members who remain committed to their church leadership ministry while also trying to recover from their own grief and hurt from whatever the situation may be.

BARRIER 2: The reason for "becoming a better church board" is unclear. Some boards make informal self-assessments and decide things are going just fine. I've found this situation to be one of the biggest barriers to growth and improvement. It's not that the board is against taking steps to improve. Rather, the board members—as a whole—aren't convinced that growth is necessary. Using Simon Sinek's mantra, they haven't been able to "Answer the Why."

In short, they can't see the reason for it, so they passively decide it's unnecessary. *This might sound worse than it actually is.* It's important to remember that many church board members are often already volunteering in several other areas of their church, such as teaching Sunday school, helping in the kids ministry, caring for the property, etc., in addition to full-time jobs and community involvement. Not to mention they care for their marriage, family and home. They're busy with very important things, and it's easy to say *"If it ain't broke, don't fix it!"* But board members often can't properly evaluate if it truly "ain't broke" from a biblical perspective. And if it is, they don't entirely know how to fix it—and therefore don't have the motivation or just can't see the reason to do so.

Here are a few other barriers that church boards encounter:

- **Institutional Memory.** This happens when board members have served for many years—or even decades—and just continue to do the same thing over and again: "This is the way we've always done it."
- **Unawareness.** Church boards are unaware of how to evaluate themselves, what improvement looks like, or that there's even such a thing as a Bible-based church board design.
- *A Strong Voice.* Sometimes, there is a member who has a strong voice, and the other board members defer to that person. This works in the

board's favor if that one person has a Bible-based commitment in their board leadership style and a Christ-focused commitment in their life and relationships. But if not, this person can cause frustration and division, often resulting in silence from the other board member, or a board environment where no one desires to serve with them. When that person's voice is the final authority, growth or improvement only takes place with their blessing and permission.

The Decision-Making Process

Another phenomenon (or a reality that exists) within the church is **the decision-making process**. Maybe more specifically, these three questions:

- *How are decisions being made in your church?*
- *Who is responsible to make them?*
- *How are the decisions carried out?*

Confusion around how decisions are made can be one of the most significant sources of tension between the pastor and board members and between board members. Because of the potential volatility in the pastor-board relationship, addressing this primary issue *BEFORE* it becomes a problem has helped many boards avoid destructive and divisive issues within their leadership team.

What Happens When This Problem Occurs?

One of the most common outcomes of a decision-making process that is dysfunctional (it's happening wrong) or nonfunctional (it's not even happening) is the breakdown of trust. Trust is the one element in a relationship that is essential to have. It takes years to build, and can take a few seconds to destroy, and it becomes endangered when decisions are made illegitimately or inappropriately. It can seem like a small issue, but when the decision made impacts something significant (hiring or firing, church discipline, budgets, etc.), members begin to point fingers and departure decisions are considered.

How Does This Problem Occur?

One of the most common causes of tension with decision-making is when transitions are made in the role of pastor, or when board roles change. Here are hypothetical examples of these causes:

> **Church A:** The long-term pastor just retired after several decades. Especially in his later years, he allowed the board to direct the key decisions about staffing, budgets, ministries, and congregational needs. This freed him up to do things he loved while supporting the board's decisions. But when a new pastor arrived—who clearly had capacity and interest to be involved in the decision-making process—it got messy.

> **Church B:** The board members had high expectations of the pastor to lead the church, and they gave him responsibilities of both making decisions and carrying them out. As long as things stayed calm, this process seemed to work. But when things became a challenge in the church, the board questioned how decisions were being made.

In both scenarios, the potential problems became an issue during times of change or challenge—and a change or challenge is always around the corner for every church. By having clear decision making processes, a church can operate nimbly and effectively. Like a prize-fighter, a church can be prepared to move smartly, effectively, and protectively when problems arise.

This situation became abundantly clear during the COVID-19 pandemic. Many churches were unprepared for the problems that the pandemic created or illuminated. The tension between pastors and boards became so significant that the "Great Resignation" followed: pastors left, and many have not returned to ministry even several years later.

How does your church leadership make decisions?

At the risk of oversimplifying a complex process, I want to suggest to you that every church that has ever existed falls into one of the these four categories:

TYPE A: Empowered Pastor, Supportive Board

TYPE B: Empowered Pastor, Empowered Board

TYPE C: Supportive Pastor, Supportive Board

TYPE D: Supportive Pastor, Empowered Board

By Empowered, I mean the designated element in a church leadership team where final decisions are made. By Supportive, I mean the designated element in a leadership team that supports the decisions.

Take a look at the following chart to see this concept laid out in the form of a rubric, and continue reading through this chapter to learn which decision-making types are the most effective to help build a healthy church leadership team.

CHURCH LEADERSHIP TYPES AND DECISION-MAKING SYSTEMS

TYPE A	**TYPE B**
Empowered Pastor, Supportive Board *Pastor's role:* Making decisions *Board's role:* Providing support **Leadership condition:** The Pastor functions as the decision-making authority; the Board assists with the Pastor's decisions.	**Empowered Pastor, Empowered Board** *Pastor's role:* Making decisions *Board's role:* Making decisions **Leadership condition:** Both the Board and the Pastor are making decisions; there is confusion and overlap with decisions and follow-through.
TYPE C	**TYPE D**
Supportive Pastor, Supportive Board *Pastor's role:* Providing support *Board's role:* Providing support **Leadership condition:** Neither the Board nor the Pastor are making decisions; Conditions can be stagnant.	**Supportive Pastor, Empowered Board** *Pastor's role:* Providing support *Board's role:* Making decisions **Leadership condition:** The Board functions as the decision-making authority; the Pastor carries out the decisions made by the Board.

Vertical axis: Leader Strength (− to +)
Horizontal axis: Board Strength (− to +)

- **TYPE A: Empowered Pastor, Supportive Board**
  This type of leadership is dependent on a pastor who can make decisions and communicate them appropriately to the board.

- **TYPE B: Empowered Pastor, Empowered Board**
  While this type of leadership might recognize the leadership gifts of both the board and the pastor, it often does not create clear boundaries in the decision-making process; frustrating for all involved.

- **TYPE C: Supportive Pastor, Supportive Board**
  This type of leadership takes place when neither the pastor nor the board are capable or empowered to make decisions; frustrating for all involved.

- **TYPE D: Supportive Pastor, Empowered Board**
  This type of leadership is dependent on the board that can make decisions and communicate them appropriately to the pastor.

Recognizing the leadership style and decision-making process of your board is a starting place. Then, consider these next steps:

1) **Consistency.** Ensure the process you use matches with the process described in the church's bylaws. This consistency is essential for unity within the board and with the pastor.

2) **Clear communication.** Ensure you clearly define the process to the board and the pastor. Clear communication about how decisions are made mitigates confusion and frustration.

3) **Adjustments.** It is possible for there to be a blend of types based on the decisions that need to be made. For example, church discipline decisions are deferred to the board, etc.). Again, consistency and clear communication is essential.

What decision-making types help create healthy church leadership teams?

So, is there a style that is best for a church board? Based on my experience, the answer is Yes—depending that each of the three above steps are being followed.

The most effective types (TYPE A and TYPE D): Followed properly, both types have clear decision-making processes that are complemented by empowered leaders.

The least effective types (TYPE B and TYPE C): Both of these types create tension and are prone to frustration and burn-out by both the pastor and the board.

For you to have a hands-on learning effort to better understand the decision-making and leadership style within your church's leadership team, I have created a self-led *Church Leadership Types and Decision-Making Systems* (CLT/DMS) Survey and Assessment Instrument. This tool has helped pastors and church boards to develop a healthy conversation about how decisions are made in their leadership team, and to consider ways to sharpen and strengthen that important process. (You can access this tool at our website – www.churchboardresources.com.)

I want to encourage you. Church boards—even ones with big barriers—can indeed pursue and improve in becoming a biblically-focused church board. It's never too late!

As the old saying goes, *"the best day to plant a tree is 10 years ago—and the second-best day to plant it is today."* Let's start building a healthy biblical church board today.

Resources for You

Suggestion on how to evaluate and improve your church board:

I recommend church board members utilize the **Church Leadership Types and Decision-Making Systems (CLT/DMS) Survey and Assessment** (found at www.churchboardresources.com) to evaluate your leadership and decision-making process, as well as to work through in your growth and development efforts.

Your notes:

3

CHURCH BOARDS: THEY NEED TO BE BETTER! (PART 1)

TIP #3

UNDERSTAND YOUR CHURCH'S ORGANIZATIONAL STRUCTURE – AND STRENGTHEN IT!

Churches are in trouble. Of course, that's nothing new. In the letters from the apostles Paul and John to the churches they helped plant, we can see that problems in the church have always existed. (*Just for clarity* – When I refer to "the church" I mean the local churches around the world that mankind is involved in, not the "Church, the Body of Christ" that is divinely led and ordained by God through His Son.)

But I deeply and fully believe in the church, and I love it dearly, particularly the small churches under 200 people—even with all the nuances, problems, and troubles. I have dedicated most of my adult life to being part of it. I am passionate about the leadership teams in small churches, and I'm not about to give up on the local church, no matter how much trouble it's in. So the tools found in this book are developed from years of learning and serving and prayerfully supporting small churches and their boards.

This chapter addresses the key issue of structure with which church boards typically struggle, where they should focus their energy on to either prevent problems, and how to recover from problems which have already occurred.

The Tension of Organizational Structure

Scripture defines the organizational structure of the church to be different. Holy and set apart. Something special. While there is nothing written in the Bible that says ALL organizations must be organized like the church, the description given to us by God in His Word (see the books suggested at the end of Chapter 1 in this book) shows a very significant organizational structure prescribed by God.

Scripture defines the organizational structure of the church to be different. Holy and set apart. Something special.

Theologians and denominations have arguments with this topic. As expected, anywhere there's a definite YES, someone will find a definite NO. But my intention is to provide clarity to an issue for many churches: the organizational structure or model of their church.

Let's start here: The typical for-profit and nonprofit organization follows a common and historical structure of a pyramid, with the small group of leaders (the board and the CEO) at the top of the pyramid, then each of the layers are filled with members of the executive team, mid-level leaders and managers, and line-level supervisors. Then at the bottom layer of the pyramid are the employees and volunteers.

Typical For-Profit and Nonprofit Organizational Structure

- CEO & Board
- Executive Team
- Mid-Level Directors and Managers
- Line-Level and Shift Supervisors
- Employees and Volunteers

Regardless of the size of the organization, this pyramid design is a practical model to help the organization accomplish its primary mission, whether it be for-profit or non-profit. This design represents not only a reflection of the actual number of people in each of those categories relative to each other (for example, there's only one CEO and a few board members, but there are many employees and volunteers), but also the top-down method for decision-making. There have been variations of this pyramid structure, but even with countless alterations, ultimately the organizations end up functioning like this pyramid illustrated above. This is true for all sorts of organizations—the military, manufacturing, education, social services, healthcare, retail, construction services and trades, etc.—not just churches.

To this end, many, if not most churches, both big and small around the world have adapted to a similar version of the pyramid-shaped organizational structure in their authority and decision-making process.

Typical (Non-Biblical) Church Organizational Structure

In certain international churches, there is a group of community or tribal elders who also are part of the top layers.

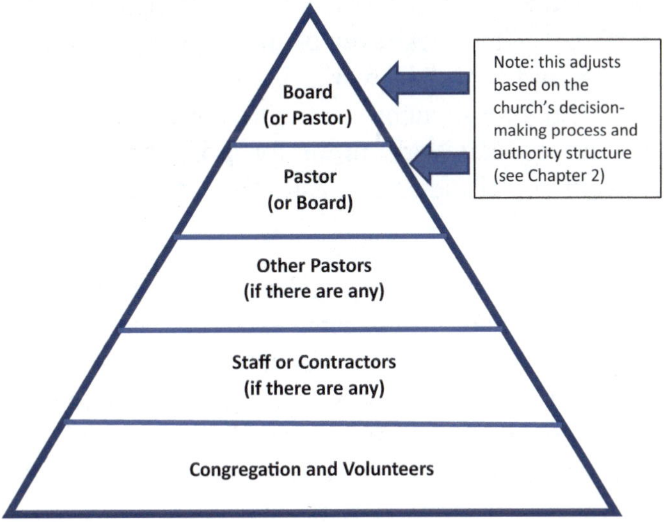

Board
(or Pastor)
Pastor
(or Board)
Other Pastors
(if there are any)
Staff or Contractors
(if there are any)
Congregation and Volunteers
Note: this adjusts based on the church's decision-making process and authority structure (see Chapter 2)

Curiously and clearly, these two pyramid-types of organizational designs are similar for a variety of reasons. Some of the reasons for their similarities stem from the spread of the church across the world and how organizations were designed and duplicated during that spread. Church-planters and missionaries created or developed what they knew. Not a criticism, just a statement of the reality. Organizational habits are typically firmly established and difficult to break.

Another reason this model is still in use throughout churches today is that most church leaders still have jobs in the marketplace (board members, dual-vocational pastors, etc.). Those leaders bring what they know into church leadership and their teams follow a structure they're familiar with.

Something Better

We need to work on breaking and eliminating this pyramid-shaped organizational model in our churches and build something completely different. Radically different—if we desire our churches to impact families, communities, and the world. The pyramid organization is not necessarily unbiblical. It's a construct that works (or at least can work) in the for-profit, nonprofit, and governmental industries. **But it's not meant for the church.**

Yes, the board members and pastor, the support staff members and volunteers, are all part of the organizational model. But rather than a model that has a pyramid type of top-down design and function, or a geometric design, let's go back to Scripture. God's Word has given us divine guidance as we consider how a church should function, and the design its organizational structure should resemble.

> *The body as a model for church organization and function is the only organizational model that truly makes sense for the church.*

The Body. Throughout the New Testament, the metaphor of a body is used repeatedly to describe the Church—The Body of Christ. For most believers, this is not a new concept or thought. But we have continued to use different models for our church's organizational structure. Yes, we see Christ as our head (Eph. 5:23), but then our churches fall back into the practical pyramid structure.

The body as a model for church organization and function is the only organizational model that truly makes sense for the church. All other shapes and designs that organizational theorists have suggested for the nonprofit and for-profit industries fall short for how the church is ordained by God and defined to function.

Metaphors are meant to give us a basic idea of something that is complex. So a logical question sounds something like this: "Yes, I understand how the Body of Christ, the Universal Church, functions with Christ as our head…but how does my local church function like that?"

To see how the body can be both the organizational model and not just a metaphor, let's break it down into two simple categories: The Unseen and the Seen. There are parts of the body we can plainly see (the Seen), and there are parts that cannot be seen or revealed without an expert, a machine, or trauma (the Unseen).

The Unseen. Our internal organs, bones, muscles, tendons, fluids, nerves, and other parts of our physiology are largely unseen. It goes without saying in detail how important those parts of our body are. Yes, we can go without a few of them if needed, and some break, tear, or are otherwise damaged, but to be truly healthy, every unseen part is important to the whole body. Each part has a function and there is no unimportant or more important part.

The Seen. The visible parts of our body—like skin, limbs, facial features, basic shape—can often appear more important. Many people determine the condition of their own health by looking at themselves in the mirror. *Well, I look healthy, so yeah, I'm healthy.* We look in the mirror dozens of times each week to get that perspective. However, we typically only see our physician (who can actually look at our unseen parts) once a year, and that doctor can see if we're truly healthy or not.

The following chart gives ideas of the model's design. Remember that in Scripture's body metaphor, Christ is the head (Eph. 1:22, 5:23; Col. 1:18; 1 Cor. 11:3). Staying within that metaphor, Christ's followers serve as members of His body, doing the work together and coordinated (Note: This chart is just an example of how a church could associate their structure with a body).

An Example of a Church Organizational Model Following the Body Metaphor

	Body Part	**How it functions in the church**	**Who or what does it refer to in the church**
The "Unseen"	Circulatory System	Strengthens and purifies	Pastor and Elder(s)
	Tendons	Ensuring unity and care	Deacons
	Muscles	Lifting up of others	Encouraging Ministry
	Nervous System	Ensuring biblical integrity	Pastor and Elder(s)
The "Seen"	Fingers	Taking care of the details	Administrative
	Skin	Protecting	Safety Team
	Eyes	Seeing the needs	Visitation Ministry
	Mouth	Leading praise	Worship Ministry
	Ears	Hearing the needs	Counseling Ministry
	Arms	Carrying the needs	Finance Ministry

	Legs	Carrying the Gospel	Evangelism
	Hands	Serving the congregation	Service Ministry
	Feet	Property stewardship	Work Team

You can see how some of the functions are up front and visible in the church's ministry, while others take place more subtly, behind the scenes. But each element is essential.

As this chart above describes the idea of a body-type of organizational structure, this picture below is a graphic that gives a more practical look at this concept.

In this design, and what we know of bodies, there are priority-level needs, especially when the body is in trauma (or when our church is in crisis). But on a daily healthy basis, every part of our body must be functioning well and to its fullest purpose. That's when things just feel right. When things in our body aren't feeling or functioning well, it's obvious to the entire body that something is wrong.

More like this

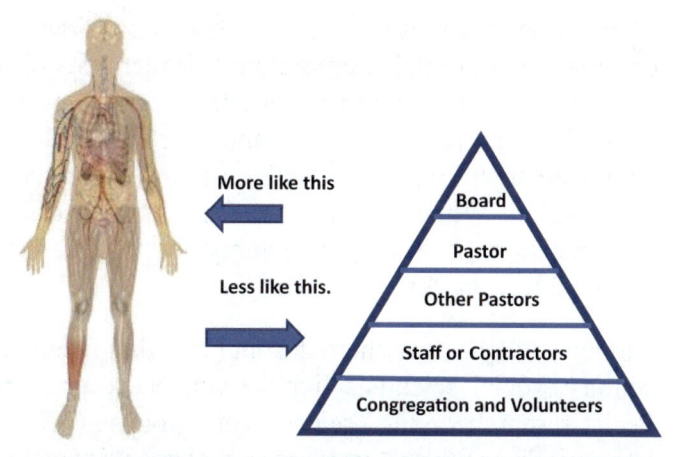

Less like this.

- Board
- Pastor
- Other Pastors
- Staff or Contractors
- Congregation and Volunteers

One could argue that all organizations are essentially like a body, or at least should aspire to be. They're not wrong—but I would suggest that many other models also work for those non-church organizations, depending on their organization's purpose, industry, location, culture, history, and countless other factors. The same can't be said for churches. **No other model can (or should) really work for a church**. The body is and should be the primary organizational model for the church.

Healthy Tension

By using the word *tension*, I don't mean something negative. My good friend explained the word using a trampoline example. In a backyard trampoline, there are little steel springs attached around the entire circle of the trampoline at regular, short intervals, hooking the jumping mat to the frame. Those springs hold that mat in a constant state of tension—stretching it tight, each in its own direction. In this example, tension is proper and healthy, and is an integral part of the trampoline's design.

There is healthy tension in a church as it considers its organizational model. Some church leaders desire to scrub any notion of corporate or organizational design from their church's function and work to make it simply an organic existence without edges, order, rules, or intention. While I appreciate that altruistic effort, human history has shown it's simply not possible for a sustainable, long-term period of time.

Among many researchers throughout the twentieth century, social scientists like Lewin, Hackman, and Peck researched the science of groups ("Group Dynamics") and the natural tendency of people to gather, eventually creating levels of leadership, structure, and purpose. Whether you're looking at a business, a small church, a school playground, or even a remote tribe in the Amazon rainforest, organizational structure happens when people gather.

So healthy tension exists in a church when we ask the question, *"Should we have an organizational structure?"* Yes. Your church does and will have an organizational structure, even if you attempt to reject it. It gets more complicated when we ask the question, *"What structure should we use?"* If we ignore this question, church leaders will inevitably and unintentionally adopt some type of organizational model, and in most cases, it ends up functioning like a pyramid. Referring back to that trampoline example, the tension that exists as we consider our church and its organizational structure is important, maybe even necessary.

The organizational structure of our church helps to keep it mission-focused, accountable to our congregation and community, and in order. We shouldn't fight against structure—because it's simply going to exist in some form. Rather, we must build and embrace the proper structure.

Resources for You

Where to Start: Three Big "If's".

#1. If you're intrigued by the conversation about organizational structure, and

#2. if you see your church has a pyramid-shaped (or other conventional metaphor) type of leadership design and function, and

#3. if you're committed to changing your church's organizational model to reflect that of a body…

…Then there's hard work ahead, but it is absolutely worth the effort.

At the risk of making a very complex process seem simple, here are a few important starting points.

First, it requires a serious evaluation of your church's organizational structure and function. Include your entire leadership team in this assessment to ensure unity in your findings. Ask questions like "Are there people or groups in our church which are more important or essential than others?" and "Does everyone in our church have an essential role to play and engage themselves into?"

Second, examine the concept of the body as the organizational structure of your church, then creatively designate what parts of the body correspond to the people, ministries, and elements of your church. Be certain to consider everyone—their gifts, interests, and abilities—and determine how they are part of your church's community and function. This means the design is dependent on specific people. If they leave or are away from the church, your body will miss them, and might even need to reorganize occasionally.

Third, involve each member of your church family. Help them define and use their gifts and educate them in how essential they are in the organizational structure and design of your church, giving them resources and mentoring to become their best.

And **fourth**, work diligently to not return to the organizational model your church once followed. Your church's muscle-memory will want to go back to those different tasks and processes that are comfortable and familiar. This might require rewriting your church's bylaws to create bumpers that will guide your leadership process.

As we look at church, God's grace allows us to function in whatever way we choose. Through his prevenient grace (His eternal will and work), His will is going to take place for His good purpose. But God has graciously given us both instructions (Scripture) and a model to follow (His Son, Jesus Christ) to help us understand and practically live out His will. Can we structure our church in whatever way we desire or in the way which we believe God is leading us and can God still use it for His will and purpose? Of course. But in church, if we follow God's design rather than our own, He will bless it because of our dedication and obedience to Him.

Leading a biblical church is not a mystery. God has defined it and designed it for us in His Word. Let us all seek to follow His design just as dedicatedly as we seek to follow His will.

License: Man shadow anatomy illustration. Public Domain: No Known Copyright

Your notes:

4

CHURCH BOARDS – THEY NEED TO BE BETTER! (PART 2)

✝

> ### TIP #4
>
> STRENGTHEN YOUR ATTITUDE ABOUT THE PRIVILEGE OF SERVING IN CHURCH LEADERSHIP.

Now that we've looked at board function, decision-making, and organizational models, the next key question is this: *How does your board interact with your congregation?*

In this chapter, we'll look more closely at the different ways board members engage with their leadership role and their congregation.

Unfortunate Attitudes

It is a great privilege and honor to serve and shepherd God's people with others who are called to do the same. At the same time, it can be heavy, repetitive, and discouraging. Unfortunately, it is easy to let unhelpful attitudes creep in. Here are some of these common attitudes. Are there any you recognize in yourself or your team?

- **The Boys Club**—This type of church board tends to be a group of men who have served together for many years. Meetings feel more social than functional—in fact, it might be seen more like the church's men's ministry.
- **The Work Team**—This type of church board keeps busy by doing the necessary tasks to keep the church in working order and well maintained. They're busy mowing the grass, painting the walls, and doing the important work of stewardship.
- **The Busy Executives**—This church board is comprised of the key leaders within the church, and they view themselves as the church's key leaders. From the outside looking in, the congregation knows the board members are making the decisions at the church.
- **The Life Sentence**—These men act and feel as if their role is not only keeping the church alive, but they also feel like if they ever step off the board, their church would probably collapse. They're serving for life, and they're not thrilled about it.

A frog in the boiling pot? This old saying sounds a bit gruesome and inhumane, but if we can get beyond that it describes something that starts off fine or even good and turns into something not so good (at least for the frog). Whether or not this process accurately describes the way to cook a frog, the analogy is if you want to boil a live frog, you can't have the water boiling from the start because the frog will jump right out when you drop it in the boiling pot. Instead, the saying implies that we should put the frog in a pot with cold water, then turn the flame on and, and while the frog swims around comfortably, the water starts to get hot gradually.

Then, as the water gets dangerously hot, the frog won't realize it's being boiled until it's too late. I'm not really sure that's how it would work with a real frog—I've never tried—but the analogy makes sense: Small incremental changes over time can dramatically change the original design and purpose, sometimes before we realize it.

A church board's purpose is designed to be special and impactful, set apart, a team of leaders commissioned by the congregation to do spiritually-focused work described in the bylaws. Those original leaders as described in the Apostle Paul's epistles in the New Testament were tasked to be the actively alert protectors and shepherds of the congregation, doctrine, and ministry of the church. That might even have been the original design for today's churches by its founders. But over time, the board can lose the founders' passion and purpose: roles are diminished, reasons for serving are changed, training and orientation loses its purpose, and eventually the church board can look significantly different, even becoming a reflection of those unhelpful types of boards mentioned above.

These negative attitudes often show up passively when we serve without intentionally supporting the work.

But over time, a church board's negative attitude can become quite active and obvious when its members purposefully do things with the wrong spirit or motive of serving.

Here's where it shows itself: In my research, one of the survey questions is, "*I am fine when a board meeting needs to be cancelled or postponed.*" The answer options are *true*, *more true than false*, *more false than true*, and *false*. (The survey is anonymous.) At the writing of this book, only 27% of the 300+ church board members from a variety of different churches, denominations, and regions answered *false*. In other words, almost three-quarters of board members surveyed would passively prefer to some degree that they don't need to gather with their board for a scheduled meeting and were fine with cancelled or postponed board meetings.

I totally get that. I've served on a church board for over twenty years. Those meetings were long, often after an already-long workday, when I was hungry and tired and my mind was occupied with many other things. When a church board meeting was cancelled, I was always fine with it. Even today, after all that I know about the incredible privilege and responsibility it is to serve on a church board, even when I am serving as the board *chair*, when a meeting needs to be cancelled or postponed, I must intentionally and prayerfully realign my mind and heart: it is a blessing to serve!

Let's change this and restore the joy and passion to the role of church board members in a biblical and purposeful way.

We *GET* to do this!

I admire and respect the faithful servants in the church who serve on their board. It can be a heavy burden on a person's emotions—often seeing their church's inside guts and the dark places—and is often one more thing to do in a person's long list of commitments. After all, isn't church a place for us to unwind and recharge as we go back into our homes, communities, and workplaces to be a faithful ambassador for Jesus Christ? Sometimes being in church means work—not holy rest and refreshment—especially when the church is in crisis, you've served on that board for decades, or when your personal life is so busy that finding available time for the church board is a challenge. Even still, our attitude when serving in church leadership needs to be "*I get to do this!*", not "*I've got to do this.*"

Even still, our attitude when serving in church leadership needs to be "I get to do this!", not "I've got to do this."

As I meet with churches across the country, I find church board members who carry a "tiredness of the soul," as described by Eugene Peterson in his book, *The Contemplative Pastor* (1993). Beyond carrying a negative attitude toward the work and service, we can begin to lose our creative energy and our thoughtful compassion, two essential characteristics in the ministry of church leadership.

Serving with a posture of a positive attitude. While it takes more than a positive attitude for us to be a ready and faithful servant, a positive attitude is the bedrock or foundation as we lead and serve. People watch their leaders and often base their own attitudes on what they observe in those who are in leadership positions. As we get the privilege of serving God's people, the posture I ask board members to take is: "I *GET* to do this, I don't *GOT* to do this." (Excuse the bad grammar.) Serving with this posture places our mindset on the reality that it's often hard work, but we can be grateful for the opportunity to be part of serving alongside the pastor and Christ-focused leaders to shepherd and care for God's people. That intentional attitude is contagious, and your congregation will be blessed and encouraged by it.

Leaders in a church set the temperature of the culture within the church. You are likely an experienced leader in your own right: in your family, your workplace, and in your community. It should not be a revelation to you that leaders have significant influence on those around them.

But as a leader in your church, your attitude toward service and the opportunity of being part of the board, even in those tough times, must be positive toward the work and privilege of that role. The people around you know the challenges of service, even if they're not part of the board. Serving with the music ministry, the nursery, the congregational care, the facilities management, etc., all require time and energy, especially when those tasks are short on volunteers (which is often the case). Bottom line: Serving others can be challenging.

With this in mind, you should be performing a regular self-check about your attitude. If your ministry of church leadership doesn't bring you joy, if late-night meetings are a constant burden, if you've lost the love of caring for and shepherding God's people, then it's time for you to consider taking a rest. Refresh your attitude and pray about how you can re-invigorate your positive attitude to the ministry of church leadership.

Personally speaking, I have done this very thing. While serving on the board of my church has been a true joy for me through the decades, I've also had times where my attitude was negative— sometimes even praying that meetings would be cancelled so I wouldn't miss time with my family. Or—I'm not proud of this, but honestly, at times I would have rather watched a Monday Night Football game than serving Jesus with a group of godly men. My attitude needed a rest and refreshment. Several times, my pastor and fellow board members were gracious to let me step away and rest. Those times were important for me.

In fact, even as I write this book, I am in a season of rest from serving on my church board. However, because I care so deeply for my pastors and fellow board members, I make sure to have regular one-on-one meetings and meals with the members of our board to pray with, encourage, and fellowship with them on a regular basis. I am still on the leadership team, just in a different seat.

Your Board and Your Congregation

One of your board's primary roles is to serve the congregation. While this seems wholly obvious, I have found that board members can lose sight of that role. The board can become a sort of boys club that gathers regularly, often for many years or decades, doing the work they're used to doing. But somehow they miss their roles as shepherds and protectors of the congregation alongside the pastor. It's not an intentional outcome, but over years, their ministry on the church board has turned into that unfortunate reality.

To mitigate the risk of this type of evolution of your board, it's important to have a clear understanding of the board's purpose and how it's meant to interact with the congregation. Leading a church is complicated. So much so that God used metaphors (The Body, Shepherding, etc.) to help us understand it. In complicated things, I appreciate some visual aids. Consider this progression of overlapping diagrams.

The Pastor/Board/Congregation Progression Model

First, let's start with the lead PASTOR. His role in the church is to shepherd and lead.

From here, we add the BOARD MEMBERS, as they interact with each other and as they support and serve *with* the pastor.

Now we add the CONGREGATION.

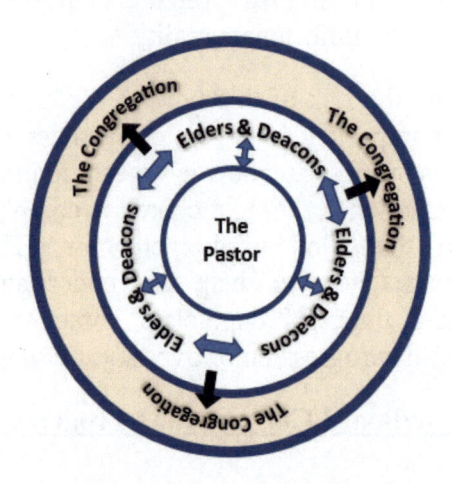

As the board works together with the pastor, the pastor-board team works to **serve, protect and shepherd** the congregation.

So the next question is what is the church's role? The answer to that is even more complex as we learn more about God's heart and will for His people and how the Church is His vessel to spread the Gospel across the world. To help us understand this question, God gives us a very clear metaphor: **A light in the darkness**.

This metaphor of a light is a common image throughout Scripture: The Psalmists provide a variety of introductions to this light metaphor; Isaiah gives us a glimpse of the image (Isa. 9:2); Christ talks about it throughout the Gospels; and the Apostle Paul uses that same metaphor in his letters to the Christians throughout the ancient Mediterranean region (2 Cor. 4:6, 6:14, 1 Thess. 5:5). Luke, a disciple of Jesus, uses it throughout the book of Acts (Acts 13:47-48, 26:16-18), as do other writers across the Old and New Testament books. The light in the darkness metaphor gives us an easy-to-grasp image of God's plan for our daily lives as devoted Christ-followers. He tells us to be a light for Him to our family, community, and to the world.

So, taking this model based on the biblical function of the church board and the purpose of the global Church, and adding the light metaphor with God and His Word as our source of power, it would be illustrated something like this in the modern day:

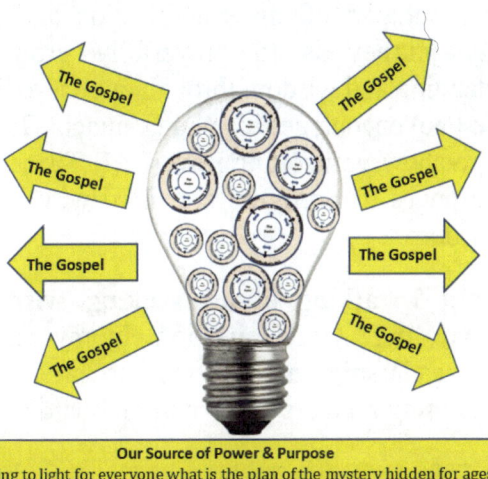

Our Source of Power & Purpose
To bring to light for everyone what is the plan of the mystery hidden for ages in God, who created all things, so that through the church the manifold wisdom of God might now be made known to the rulers and authorities in the heavenly places. This was according to the eternal purpose that he has realized in Christ Jesus our Lord (Eph. 3:9-11)

Creating a Purpose Statement for Your Board

Experts have plenty to say about the great value being informed has on our ability to engage into our work. The concept and process of making informed decisions is important in moving forward when we're faced with opportunities and options. It's no different with our service on a church board. While we'd like to think the ministry calling we've heard and responded to would supernaturally and divinely bridge all gaps in our knowledge so we could serve with confidence and boldness, that simply is not how it works.

It is our responsibility to be prepared and ready to serve God. There is no place in Scripture that states—or even implies—that God will grant divine wisdom when we answer His call and serve Him with our lives. Yes, we see in the stories of God's Word where He gives special wisdom, but part of our sanctification and spiritual-maturity journey is to prayerfully grow in our understanding and wisdom through our entire lives. The Apostle Paul encourages his young student, Timothy, to "study to show yourself approved" (II Timothy 2:15), and the pages of Scripture are filled with charges to seek wisdom.

Why am I talking about seeking wisdom and understanding? Good question. In my research of church leadership across the country, I found overwhelming realities about church board members:

- 73% of church boards do not have any orientation process for new board members.
- 86% of church board members do not have a clear understanding of their role on the board.
- 56% of church boards have no defined description of how their board functions or what a board member is supposed to do.

In light of this research, I have found that one of the easiest and essential ways forward is to create a purpose statement for their board. While this task can sound a bit business-oriented—which is not always bad, by the way—this process helps them build a clear understanding of why their board exists, how they can effectively collaborate, and what the role of each board member is so they can serve together to accomplish the work of the board.

The process of creating a purpose statement is a relatively easy—but time-consuming—effort that requires a commitment by the entire board to pursue. These are the basic steps of the process:

Step 1: Define the mission of your church. Maybe you already have a Mission Statement. Great! If not, prayerfully work together (with your pastor, board and congregation) to clarify what you believe is God's purpose for your church—toward your congregation, your community, and the world. With a firm understanding of your church's purpose and mission, the next step is to determine how the board can help focus the church on that mission.

- *Pro-Tip*: Each church has its own passion and focus. With prayer, and in collaboration with your entire church, refine your church's passion into two or three key statements. What are the two or three things that drive our church family and define what we prayerfully desire to see God do in and through us in our congregation, community, and the world?

Step 2: Determine how the board fits into your church's mission. With your church's Mission Statement now defined, it's time to understand and clarify how the church board must lead and shepherd the congregation toward that mission.

- *Pro-Tip:* For example, if in your church's Mission Statement is a guiding goal to have healthy and vibrant Christ-following marriages and families, then you might decide as a board that your church will be dedicated to Sunday School for all ages providing consistent opportunities to study Scripture, build meaningful relationships, and pursue spiritual growth. Therefore, an essential part of the church board's Purpose Statement must include a commitment to building and maintaining the Sunday School program (teaching, finding volunteers, deciding upon curriculum, etc.).

Step 3: Define your church board's Purpose Statement. Once you have defined your church's Mission Statement, and you've determined what the board's role is in that mission, now create a *concise* statement that clarifies the board's role in your church.

- *Pro-Tip*: For a church with a Mission Statement that reads "Our church is passionate about and will prayerfully pursue healthy, vibrant families and marriages that diligently seek Christ, reach our community to faithfully show God's grace and Christ's love with care and compassion, and support the sharing of the Gospel around the world in meaningful and impactful ways." Now, your board can create a clear Purpose Statement that supports and guides each of those mission goals.

A church board which has a clear Purpose Statement can then create role descriptions for each of the board members which will help the board accomplish its purpose within the church. The church board then **partners** with the congregation in pursuing the church's mission and **shepherds** the congregation toward its mission. This clarity of the partnership between the board and the congregation is especially important when a church encounters crises and hardship.

Resources for You

One of the most helpful and supporting tools that we've provided for churches across the country is the **Church Assessment Rubric** (you can find this Rubric at www.churchboardresources.com). This document helps you and your board to do the following:

- Assess your board (It is working well? Does it properly meet the needs of your church? Is it following a biblical model? etc.).
- Determine key growth areas your board desires to invest in and what to prioritize.
- Create tools to help address those key items.

You can go to our website for the Church Assessment Rubric.

<u>Your notes:</u>

5

SPIRITUAL MATURITY AND CHURCH LEADERSHIP

TIP #5

INVEST YOURSELF INTO INTENTIONALLY GROWING IN YOUR SPIRITUAL MATURITY AS A CHURCH LEADER.

Here's the thing: **our spiritual maturity** is possibly the most vital building block for church leaders to invest in daily. Church leaders must embrace a deep understanding of spiritual maturity. In my doctoral research, I surveyed church leaders about the biblical concept and description of spiritual maturity, and most could not provide even the most basic of definition or examples.

As a church leader, there is a direct connection between our spiritual maturity and the health of our pastor and church. I can't think of a more important investment of your brain power and prayer power than to grow in spiritual maturity—for your marriage, family, ministry, workplace, and community.

> *As a church leader, there is a direct connection between our spiritual maturity and the health of our pastor and church.*

As you balance the many roles in your life, this effort to focus on spiritual growth and maturity can be easily overlooked. It's more than just spending time in the Word, fellowshipping with other believers, and praying amid a busy life. In fact, it requires us to slow to a peaceful pace to concentrate on hearing God's voice in our life.

The Doctrine of Sanctification

Let's first look at the doctrine of sanctification and its foundational role in spiritual maturity. The theological concept of sanctification presents Christians with the challenge to view life as a process of seeking holiness in all things and then dedicating all aspects of their life to achieving holiness (Allen, 2017). The doctrine of holiness in its most simple perspective speaks to a Christ-centered perspective of ethics (Allen, 2017).

To understand the concept of holiness, we simply must study Jesus Christ (Van De Walle, 2017). The Holy God demonstrated for humanity what holiness is in the incarnation of Jesus Christ (John 1:14). He became Immanuel, "God with us" (Matthew 1:23 ESV). In addition to being the model and example of holiness, Christ is also the means (Hebrews 13:12) whereby mankind can become holy, through his death and resurrection (Van De Walle, 2017).

There is healthy debate among Christian scholars across denominations about the doctrine of sanctification (Gundry et al., 1998; Kolb & Trueman, 2017; Maxwell, 1997). But most scholars agree sanctification is a lifelong pursuit that involves total immersion into the study and imitation of the life of Christ. It is also important to acknowledge that sanctification is no easy pursuit; in Luke 14:25-33 Jesus says it would be a heavy burden (v.27), would require deep sacrifice (v.33), and that the love of God would be like no other love (v.26) (Sanders, 1962).

Sanctification is the theological doctrine that requires all Christ-followers to use Christ and his life as the standard of living and as the base of all ethics and decisions (Gill, 2017; Nass & Kreuer, 2018; Wilkens, 2017). While it is debated if a Christ-follower can achieve complete sanctification prior to Glory, Scripture is clear: it is God's will for people to relentlessly pursue sanctification (1 Thessalonians 4:3-5, 2 Peter 3:18, Hebrews 12:14); God has provided the means of sanctification (1 John 1:9, Philippians 2:13, Hebrews 10:10, 12:1); and the pursuit of sanctification continues until the day Christ returns (Ephesians 4:13, Philippians 1:6).

The Doctrine of Spiritual Maturity

Understanding the doctrine of spiritual maturity provides practical insight into sanctification. The question that eventually must be examined is, "What does sanctification produce?" Or more precisely, "What does a Christ-follower's life look like when they are pursuing sanctification?" In Scripture, the theme of "growing up" is often used to describe the life of a Christ follower (Boa, 2001) and refers to the stages of sanctification throughout life (Chandler, 2014).

Christ describes this process as he preached to the crowd in Matthew 5-7 in a discourse known as the Sermon on the Mount, or the Beatitudes. In what Sanders (1962) refers to as "Christ's ideal of character" (p.365), he divides the first eight attributes of Christ's sermon (Matthew 5:3-11) into two sections: the first four verses (vs. 3-6) refer to how Christ-followers view God, and the last four verses (vs. 7-11) refer to how Christ-followers view others. This provides a framework for the ethics and attitudes God desires for his people to desire and pursue (Cloud, 2006). "Such is our Lord's lofty concept of Christian character" (Sanders, 1962, p. 370).

Spiritual maturity can be viewed as the process of change that occurs in a person when they understand and pursue the values, traits, and attitudes of Christ (S. Porter, 2019). Maturing spiritually is a life-long pursuit that involves the very core of a person's character, how they view others and God, and how they interact with those relationships (Sanders, 1962) (Willard, 2016).

Spiritual Fruit

As a follower of Christ diligently seeks sanctification, there is an outcome in a person's life: Spiritual fruit (Matthew 7:15-20, Galatians 5:22-23, Ephesians 5:9). Love, joy, peace, patience, kindness, goodness, faithfulness, gentleness, self-control (Galatians 5:22-23), power (2 Timothy 1:7), humility (Colossians 3:12), compassionate hearts, and meekness (Ephesians 4:2).

The concept of fruitfulness is found throughout the entirety of Scripture as it describes the attributes of God (Weems & Berlin, 2011). From God's interaction with Abraham in Genesis (17:6) to His final words to John in Revelation, (Revelation 22:2), the concept of God's work always producing his desired outcome is woven throughout Scripture.

However, not all growth in character and its subsequent outcome is a supernatural process (S. Porter, 2019). Indeed, it is a natural assumption that a person, regardless of if they are a Christ-follower, may experience character growth if they set their mind on good things. But, the presence of the Holy Spirit is a clear distinction between a person who does not follow Christ and one who believes Jesus is God's son who died and then resurrected (Romans 10:9-10) (Weems & Berlin, 2011). The Holy Spirit's presence ensures the supernatural outcomes of spiritual fruit as a Christ-follower seeks God. In contrast, a non-believer in Christ may or may not grow in their ethics and character even though that might be the focus of their being. Weems & Berlin (2011) say "one might reasonably expect given this Christian view of things that being inhabited by the Spirit of a morally perfect God would make a morally significant difference in one's life" (p.120, para.2).

Additionally, not all Christ-followers can claim they have experienced the life-change described in Scripture, nor have they witnessed the spiritual fruit that comes with it. The absence of the fruit in their life can act as a critique against the promises of God in Scripture and negatively shape their beliefs as a Christ-follower. People might profess their faith in Jesus Christ but not display the characteristics of a changed life or the fruit that comes with a life that is maturing spiritually with God. This is a difficult situation and one requiring self-assessment to determine the reason for this predicament (Weems & Berlin, 2011).

Another unique characteristic about spiritual fruit is it's used as a measurement by Jesus Christ for the Church (Addington, 2010). Christ states, "This is to my Father's glory, that you bear much fruit, showing yourselves to be my disciples" and "I chose you and appointed you to go and bear fruit – fruit that will last" (John 15:8, 16). For Christ, it's the spiritual fruit that matters, not just the outcomes. The eternal fruit takes place only through the power of Jesus Christ. Addington (2010, p. 40) identifies the following evidence of spiritual fruit from the New Testament:

- People coming into a personal relationship with God (Mark 1:1-20; Luke 19:10; Philemon 6).

- A desire that Christ would change us into His likeness so we can take on His character and priorities over time (Colossians 3:1-17; 2 Peter 1:3-11).

- Becoming passionate about knowing Him through His word and through intimacy with Him in prayer (John 15; James 1:19-25).

- Obeying and following Christ in all parts of life as our highest priority (1 John 2:3-6).

- A love for others that grows and flourishes in our hearts, resulting in acts of kindness (John 15:9-17).

- Obedience to Christ that causes us to engage in changing and influencing the world around us for Him (1 Peter 2:9-12).

- Becoming people who long to see eternal fruit come from our lives (John 15:5, 16; Colossians 1:10).

- Regular growth in the display of the Spirit's fruit in us (Galatians 5:22-25).

Bottom line: spiritual maturity matters. Bearing spiritual fruit is essential, and the results are important. Christ provided a command and commission to produce results in Matthew 28:19 by stating: "Therefore go and make disciples of all nations, baptizing them in the name of the Father and of the Son and of the Holy Spirit."

Resources for You

Suggestions on how to evaluate and improve your spiritual maturity:

I recommend for church board members to utilize the **Spiritual Maturity – Self-Assessment Guide** (you can find this guide at www.churchboardresources.com) to evaluate your understanding and application of spiritual maturity, and for you and your church leadership team to work through in your spiritual maturity assessment and growth.

<u>Your notes:</u>

6

THE IDEAL RELATIONSHIP: "A MORE PERFECT UNION"

TIP #6
RISE UP – AND PRAY LIKE KING DAVID!

Long before the phrase "*A more perfect union*" was coined for the Preamble of the U.S. Constitution, Scripture clearly described the power of a unified group focused on a common goal. The idea of the pastor, board, and congregation unified in a healthy, biblical, and Christ-focused partnership, working together with other churches, is infinitely more powerful than what any government could ever design or hope to be!

There are many obstacles in the way that can prohibit this type of healthy, biblical collaboration. Knowing how much Satan hates God and humanity—and any work the Church does to bring others to a saving knowledge of God—some of those obstacles are placed by him through vicious spiritual warfare. And unfortunately, some of those obstacles we create by our own brokenness.

For both of these realities, it's important for church leaders to rise above these complications and seek ways to lead and shepherd our congregations in a biblically defined and practical way. Our goal is to be a better reflection of Christ and to equip capable ambassadors for Him to impact this world.

RISE UP – and Pray Like King David!

This boundless work of the Church that all Christ-followers have been divinely commissioned to do can be daunting, especially in a culture that rejects the Gospel, ridicules and mocks God, and even persecutes His people in an ever-increasing way. Add to that the pressures that churches face (finances, resources, governments, activists, etc.), the heartbreaking realities of life (broken marriages, in-fighting, legalism, compromise, corruption, pastoral burn-out, etc.), and the need for church resolute and dedicated leaders, and having unity in purpose in the church, becomes clearer and more important each day.

The hard news is these growing pressures and challenges will not end until Jesus returns and we see Him face-to-face. The work of His Church on earth will be done in that moment, and for eternity, we will be praising only Him. Until that day, the hard work of the church will continue—and will get harder.

But there is good news, too! This isn't the first time things seemed hopeless or unreachable for God's people. History is full of stories where God preserved His people through His divine grace, equipping them to keep fighting and moving.

One of my favorite testimonies of this is in the story of David and Absalom in 2 Samuel, and then again in Psalm 3. We see King David, a man who God described as having His heart, fleeing Jerusalem (the city and kingdom he helped to build!) under siege by a revolution led by his own son, Absalom. As Absalom's army pursues his father, King David and his entourage flee to the caves and hills (2 Samuel 13:23).

In that moment, when it seemed like everything was lost and hopeless, having no chance to see God work, David stopped and prayed. In the middle of it all, he prayed—and then shared it with us in Psalm 3. More than just a prayer, though, God—through His faithful servant, David—showed us HOW to pray when things seem lost and hopeless.

Take a look at David's prayer recorded in Psalm 3, and see the pattern of this prayer for deliverance from despair:

Psalm 3 - A psalm of David. When he fled from his son Absalom.	**RISE UP!** **David's Prayer Pattern**	
1. Lord, how many are my foes! How many rise up against me! 2. Many are saying of me, "God will not deliver him."[b] 3. But you, Lord, are a shield around me, my glory, the One who lifts my head high. 4. I call out to the Lord, and he answers me from his holy mountain. 5. I lie down and sleep; I wake again, because the Lord sustains me. 6. I will not fear though tens of thousands assail me on every side. 7. Arise, Lord! Deliver me, my God! Strike all my enemies on the jaw; break the teeth of the wicked. 8. From the Lord comes deliverance. May your blessing be on your people.	**R**	Vs. 1-2 – **RECOGNIZE** the fear, concern, and hopelessness.
	I	Vs. 3 – **IDENTIFY** God's attributes and who He is.
	S	Vs. 4-5 – **STATE** aloud what you've already seen God do in and through your life.
	E	Vs. 6 – **ENCOURAGE** yourself the God's Truth and His promises.
	U	Vs. 7 – **UNARM** and pray again your fears, concerns, and anxieties.
	P	Vs. 8 – **PRAISE** God and give Him the Glory for what He has done, is doing, and will do.

Friend, this pattern of a ***RISE UP*** prayer shows us how to pray when things seem lost or hopeless. As you look ahead at your church and the work it still must do, things can feel too difficult to continue at times. When that happens, your entire church can be in danger. Pastors resign, board members quit, congregations shrink, churches close. But it doesn't have to be that way.

When we prayerfully approach the work of a church board with both a theological and biblical perspective, there is great hope and knowledge that God's work will be done in and through us. It has and always will require our best effort. We'll come up short in our work, but God **will** accomplish all that His will has determined to accomplish, through His people who love Him, according to His timing (Romans 8:28).

Resources for you.

This journey of refining your church board is not meant to be done alone. Our ministry has more resources for you (see them at our website www.churchboardresources.com), and we can walk alongside you—in person or via technology—to serve with you and your board for the long-haul. We're passionate about serving church pastors and boards. It's all we do, and we've done it for hundreds of churches across the country and internationally. We carefully count the churches we can serve so we can provide reliable one-on-one support.

Reach out to us for a chance to talk about your journey!

I am deeply moved by the faithful work of church board members. May you and your team serve with wisdom, discernment, confidence, courage, sensitivity, and compassion—and may you never cease seeking growth and development in your church board!

Let me end with this blessing as you faithfully and prayerfully serve, lead, and shepherd on your church board.

And God is able to make all grace abound to you, so that having all sufficiency in all things at all times, you may abound in every good work.

(2 Corinthians 9:8)

Your notes:

REFERENCES

Addington, T. J. (2010). High impact boards: Church boards. In *How to develop healthy, intentional, and empowered church leaders*: Book Villages.

Allen, M. (2017). *Sanctification*. HarperCollins Christian Publishing.

Boa, K. (2001). *Conformed to His image : biblical and practical approaches to spiritual formation*. Zondervan.

Chandler, D. J. (2014). *Christian spiritual formation an integrated approach for personal and relational wholeness*. Intervarsity Press.

Cloud, H. (2006). *Integrity*. HarperCollins.

Gill, R. (2017). *Moral Passion and Christian Ethics*. Cambridge University Press.

Gundry, S. N., Dieter, M. E., Hoekema, S. M. H., McQuilkin, J. R., & Walvoord, J. F. (1998). *Five views on sanctification*. HarperCollins Christian Publishing.

Kolb, R. W., & Trueman, C. R. (2017). *Between Wittenberg and Geneva : Lutheran and reformed theology in conversation*. Baker Academic.

Maxwell, A. W. (1997). *Beliefs concerning the doctrine of entire sanctification held by lay full members of the Atlantic District of the*

Wesleyan Church [Dissertation, Canadaian Theological Seminary].

Nass, E., & Kreuer, E. (2018). Methodology and applicatioins of Christian leadership ethics [6]. *The Journal of Values-Based Leadership*, *11*(2).

Porter, S. L. (2019). The evidential force of spiritual maturity and the Christian doctrine of sanctification. *Religious Studies*, *55*(1).

Sanders, J. O. (1962). *Spiritual maturity*. Moody Publishers.

Van De Walle, B. A. (2017). *Rethinking holiness : A theological introduction*. Baker Academic. ProQuest Ebook Central

Weems, L. H., & Berlin, T. (2011). *Bearing fruit*. Adingdon Press.

Willard, D. (2016). *Spiritual Formation: What it is, and How it is Done.*

Wilkens, S. (2017). *Christian Ethics: Four Views*. InterVarsity Press.

Made in the USA
Columbia, SC
10 November 2024